Case Studies

Geography, IT and the National Curriculum

This booklet should be used with the accompanying booklet
"Geography, IT and the National Curriculum".

Permissions
These booklets contain material derived from several, earlier publications. Permission to
reproduce or adapt materials from the following sources is gratefully acknowledged:
Planning I.T. in Field Studies   NCET, 1989.
Learning Geography with Computers   NCET, 1990.
Focus on I.T.   NCET, 1991.
Curriculum Council for Wales, HMSO, the Advisory Unit For Microtechnology in Education,
the Computer Based Modelling Across the Curriculum Project.

This is a joint publication between the Geographical Association and the National Council for
Educational Technology (NCET), with generous support and financial assistance from NCET.

Information Technology (I.T.) may be defined as the technology associated with the handling of information: its storage, processing and transmission in a variety of forms by electronic means, and its use in controlling the operation of machines and other devices."

(Information Technology from 5—16, Curriculum Matters 15, HMI).

The abbreviation IT is used throughout these two booklets.

Technical terms are explained in the Glossary, towards the end of the accompanying booklet
"Geography, IT and the National Curriculum".

ISBN 0 948512 30 X

Published by the Geographical Association,
343 Fulwood Road, Sheffield, S10 3BP. Telephone: 0742 670 666.

Case Studies: Contents

Introduction

Nine case studies are presented here to reflect real teaching experiences in classrooms and field centres. They are intended to be read alongside the chapters in the main booklet:'Geography, IT and the National Curriculum'. The case studies demonstrate a range of teaching and learning styles and illustrate how, in different contexts, the strands of IT capability may be integrated into geographical work.

Relevant questions and prompts for discussion are noted in the margins.

The case studies may provide a focus for discussion in your school and geography department or be used as part of LEA- and school-based INSET. Each case study identifies the type of software used and the geography and IT aims.

Each case study includes the Geography and IT Statements of Attainment that it supports and a number of ideas for further work. The case studies may be used as starting points for further IT experience or planning additional work as an INSET activity.

Finally, although the case studies here concentrate on examples from Key Stages 3 and 4, some of the ideas contained and issues addressed are relevant to those working at Key Stage 2.

Software

The software used in the case studies is, in most cases, readily available and widely tested. Packages like GRASS are content free and may already be in your school.

Software used in the Case Studies
GRASSHOPPER: available from Newman College, Birmingham.
STARS*: available from the Advisory Unit, Hatfield.
GRASS*: available from Newman College, Birmingham.
POP* data file.
CHOOSING SITES* (incl. Airport file) is published by Longman.
DEFENDING THE RAIN FOREST Project HIT, Longman, 1991.
* *Also in the NCET pack 'Learning Geography with Computers'.*

The Case Studies at a Glance

The main features of the case studies are summarised opposite. The relationship of the case studies to Geography ATs and strands of IT capability are outlined along with equipment and room requirements.

The case studies at a glance

	Title	Geography ATs	IT capability	IT application	Requirements and remarks
1	Defending the rain forest	2, 3, 4, 5	Communicating Ideas	Newsroom simulation Word processing	1 computer & printer for simulation. Computer room for WP and DTP.
2	Population and development	1, 2, 4	Information Handling	Data handling	1 computer with large screen. Computer room for follow up.
3	River study	1,2,3	Information Handling	Data handling Spreadsheet	Enquiry approach and fieldwork. 2 computers in classroom.
4	Petrol stations	4	Modelling	Simulation	Computer room.
5	Traffic in towns	2, 4	Information Handling Modelling	Spreadsheet	Enquiry approach and fieldwork. Computers at field centre.
6	Locating an airport	2, 4, 5	Applications and Effects Modelling	Geography software	2 computers in classroom.
7	Data logging: weather	1,3	Measurement and Control	Data handling Data logging	1 computer linked to data-logger. 1 or more computers for follow up.
8	Farm study	2, 4	Information Handling Modelling	Spreadsheet	Fieldwork or link with local farmer. 1 or more computers.
9	Shopping enquiry	1, 2, 4	Information Handling Communicating Ideas	Data handling DTP	Fieldwork with computers for follow up.

1 Defending the rain forest

To simulate a newsroom responding to the news of the murder of the Brazilian rubber tapper and defender of the rain forests, Chico Mendes.

Aim of study.

Geography aims:
- To raise pupil's awareness of issues involved in the rain forest of Brazil and their global implications.
- To help pupils understand that different values and attitudes exist.
- To foster co-operation and discussion within groups and to organise tasks within time constraints.

IT capability aims:
- To use IT to prepare a piece of work combining graphics and text in order to communicate information to an audience.

Software and resources:
- Simtex (Nimbus), Teletext Extra (BBC).
- Any word processing or desk top publishing package, with tables organised so pupils can work in groups.

Statements of attainment.
Places: Gg2/4c, Gg2/5c, Gg2/8d.
Physical: Gg3/6f, Gg3/8c.
Human: Gg4/4e, Gg4/7c, Gg4/8c.
Environmental: Gg5/4b, Gg5/6c, Gg5/7c, Gg5/8a, Gg5/8b, Gg5/9a, Gg5/10a.
IT capability: Te5/3a, Te5/4a, Te5/5a, Te5/6a, Te5/6a.

As an introduction to this topic, the class had already researched the background to rain forests in Brazil and the teacher had brought in a selection of newspapers and magazines as resource material. Pupils were then told the geography classroom was to become a simulated newsroom office and that a 'real' event was to be flashed to the 'telex' machine. Different newspaper styles were discussed and each group was briefed to work on a given paper or magazine.

Have pupils prior knowledge of this software?

Tasks within the groups were discussed and roles chosen. The layout of the newsroom was discussed.

Have you space for a computer with each group?

When the 40 minute lesson using IT began, the computer on the teacher's desk flashed and buzzed eleven messages onto the screen and printed out five copies of each. One reporter from each group collected the message and took it to their area of the newsroom. Two messages referred to 'faxes', with a photograph of Mendes and some longer text items; these too were collected.

Could you use the computer room?

Each group had a work area where news items were discussed and text was entered into a word processing package on the groups computer. Atlases, maps of Brazil and reference materials in the 'newsroom library' were consulted. Maps and graphics were discussed, prepared and altered as news items appeared.

Are suitable printers available for this work?

```
00.01

From: INTERNATIONAL NEWS AGENCY

23 December 1988 Xapuri,
Acre state, Brazil.

Francisco (Chico) Mendes, leader
of Brazil's rubber tappers and
internationally acclaimed defender
of the rain forest, died yesterday.
```

As follow up, the text was agreed within the group. Some groups transferred their text into a DTP package and discussion was then about layout and presentation in keeping with the style and audience of the chosen newspaper or magazine. After printing out, maps and diagrams were pasted into the spaces left for them.

As well as giving help when requested with reference materials, and prompting when required, the teacher was able to observe the pupils at work, individually and within a group.

How would you assess this group work?

In the following lessons, the five articles were displayed. Each group explained which aspects of the story they had emphasised, their choice of graphics, headlines and sub-headings. The different styles of presentation were discussed. Each group's work was later assessed for content, layout and presentation.

Going further
- Link with English lesson on the issues of bias in the reporting of information.
- Explore the issues of global warming in greater detail and the management issues related to deforestation.
- Use simulated telex messages for other contexts, such as the passing of a hurricane or a mountain rescue incident.

Source of case study.

The newsroom simulation file, pupil resources and teaching strategies are provided in DEFENDING THE RAIN FORESTS, published by Longman for Project HIT.

2 Population and development

To compare and investigate population, economic and welfare information for different parts of the world.

Aim of study.

Geography aims:

- to encourage pupils to:
  - suggest geographical questions to direct their enquiries;
  - select relevant information from secondary sources;
  - identify geographical patterns;
  - explore relationships and draw conclusions.
- to examine changes in the population sizes of different countries and possible reasons for them.

IT capability aims:

- to use IT for investigations requiring the analysis of data.

Software and resources:

- A data handling package (in this example, GRASS) and a file of population data (POP).

Statements of attainment Geographical Skills: Gg1/4e, Gg1/7e, Gg1/8c. Places: Gg2/7b. Human Geography: Gg4/5a, Gg4/6. Environment: Gg5/8a. IT capability: Te5/4d, Te5/7d.

During the course of work on population and development, it was decided to use the population datafile with GRASS to investigate some population questions. The file contains information on 65 countries and enables several lines of enquiry to be pursued by pupils, both about countries in general and about those in the programmes of study.

How can this support AT2?

One computer with a large monitor was available in the geography classroom. The software was demonstrated to the class using the record for Kenya to show the type of information held on the data file. Figures and indices were explained and investigations carried out showing:

Is prior knowledge of IT necessary?

- how sorting could find the largest and smallest countries,
- how scattergraphs could show relationships such as total population in relation to numbers of doctors.

The class were familiar with ideas of ranking and the use of scattergraphs from previous lessons.

The class then discussed what statistics could indicate a country's level of economic development and what the term 'development' itself meant. The class were then given the hypothesis that population growth rate was related to levels of economic development.

What starting points would you provide?

Working in pairs, pupils had to select three fields from the data file which they thought would illustrate whether or not a country was economically developed. They had to justify their choice and use the computer to generate and print out scattergraphs of their indicators graphed against population growth rates. (Where possible, additional computers were used for this part of the lesson).

How can you generate excitement with only one computer?

How could this be assessed?

No pair chose the same three indices and those who had time went on to look at more. Search and sort routines were also used to find out about points on graphs which did not fit any general pattern and countries were identified and located using atlases and world wall maps. Pupils then drew conclusions on how far population growth rates and economic development were linked.

This prompted further discussion on how accurate the original data in the data file might be. Pupils discovered some indices were linked closely to population change rates but there were many exceptions. Discussing reasons for the exceptions was another valuable activity.

The lessons finished with conclusions being made about the usefulness of various indices of development and how far the development of primary health care and education, in particular, related to rates of population change. This led to work on how population growth rates put pressure on resources and possibly limited levels of development.

Three important points that emerged from the lessons were:

1 The indices used to create fields in the POP data file must be clearly explained and require careful interpretation.

2 Pupils were not familiar with the location of all the countries on the file, so the lesson became one of learning about position of a country in the world and an atlas was a necessary resource.

3 Pupils enjoyed using the data file to develop their own lines of enquiry. So the computer room was booked for the follow up lesson to enable more use of the data file by the pupils.

Going Further
- Develop your own data files for particular schemes of work. One teacher wanted to look at links between a country's level of development and the status of women. As a result, fields were created for girls in secondary education and female literacy levels, to compare with figures for males in a modified GRASS POP file.
- Pupils could use the same data handling package to enter data collected on a half day's field work at a local shopping centre.

Source of case study.

Adapted from Learning Geography with Computers, NCET 1990.

3 A river case study

To look at factors which influence streamflow in a short section of stream,with the help of a data-handling package.

Aim of study.

Geography aims:
- to look at rivers in the landscape and on maps;
- to develop an understanding of changes in a river downstream and the factors that influence stream flow;
- to practice various data collection methods and evaluate their success;
- to design and evaluate methods of fieldwork data collection.

IT capability aims:
- to collect and organise data in a data handling package, and store, retrieve, analyse and present that data;
- to use search and sort methods to obtain relevant information from a database.

Software:
- data handling package such as GRASS;
- a spreadsheet, such as: GRASSHOPPER or EXCEL.

Statements of Attainment Skills: Gg1/4f, Gg1/5b, Gg1/5c, Gg1/6c, Gg1/6d. Places: Gg2/3c. Physical: Gg3/3c, Gg3/4c, Gg3/5c, Gg3/6d, Gg3/6e. IT Capability: Te5/4c, Te5/4d, Te 5/5c, Te5/6c, Te5/7d, Te5/7e, Te5/8a.

Many schools find the opportunity to carry out fieldwork tasks on rivers, usually involving collecting data on sites for hypothesis testing. The use of a simple database such as GRASS provides a ready means to collate, analyse and present such data. (There is scope to use a spreadsheet, for calculations such as river discharge).

In this example, preparatory work began with an introduction to river and valley features using postcards, slides, video images and relevant textbooks. Then a study section of a local wadeable stream was identified by the teacher and pupils studied it on a map extract and drew a simple sketch map, highlighting river and valley features visible on the map. Pupils discussed possible changes they might see as they progressed down the river section or looked across channel sections.

From this discussion, a number of hypotheses were suggested, based around the factors that influence streamflow, such as velocity will increase downstream, and channel shape will affect flow. From these the statement 'there are differences between narrow and wide channel sections' was used as the starting point for fieldwork.

What data will be needed?

Methods of data-collection were discussed, including how the pupils could design their own pieces of equipment and test their effectiveness.

Are there links here with Design and Technology?

Does use of IT influence the quantity of data that will be collected?

A fieldwork visit was then arranged to the stream. With the permission of landowners and suitable safety precautions, pupils working in groups of 3 or 4 were given study sections of stream. Each group aimed to study two sections, moving downstream. At each site they noted, recorded and observed the items listed in Table 1.

Table 1: Field observations for river case study
1. Site / Location name.
2. Distance from stream source (derived from map).
3. Width.
4. Depth every 0.5 metres across stream.
5. Wetted perimeter, using tape or weighted rope.
6. Average stream velocity (by timing a float several times).
7. Index of friction*.
8. Type of water flow (calm, rapid, turbulent, by observation).
9. Type of bed (pebbles, sand, mud, concrete, by observation).
10. Water quality*.
11. Limitations and problems which might affect results.

*   *Derived from standard textbooks on fieldwork techniques.*

Back in class, the cross-sectional area of the channel for each site was calculated, along with the discharge (velocity * area) and channel efficiency (area / wetted perimeter). Cross-sectional area can be found by plotting width and depth figures onto graph paper at a scale suggested by the teacher, but here part of the class used a pre-prepared spreadsheet, (GRASSHOPPER) to calculate the cross-sectional area, discharge and efficiency for each site. This information was then used by other groups, adding 3 more items of data to those in Table 1.

How would you organise the classroom for this work?

With up to 12 sites per class, and 4 or more items of data about each site, there is considerable data to be processed or examined. Before there was access to IT there were two alternatives. Either maps, graphs and overlays were drawn, which involved considerable time to produce and bored some pupils, or very generalised statements were made using examples of data on an OHP or blackboard. Now with IT, the data-handling package GRASS was set up for each group to enter the full list of data for their sites.

How can individual pupil work be assessed?

Once entered, the data could be analysed by the whole class, or by groups, or individual pupils, to test hypotheses. Pupils can make many varied comparisons, and they can print out graphs or tables of data.

Some hypotheses tested in this case were:

- Do narrow channels have higher velocities? (scatter graph of width against velocity).

- Do sections of stream with sandy beds flow faster than those with pebble beds? (sort velocity from high to low and print out site, velocity and type of bed).

- Does velocity increase as you go downstream? (scatter graph of velocity and distance from source).

- Is velocity related to average depth of channel section? (scatter graph of velocity and average depth of channel).

- Do channels with high friction have less discharge? (sort friction from high to low and print out site, friction score and discharge).

The use of the database made processing of data much quicker. It allowed comparisons between groups to take place. It also developed pupils' IT skills including: entering data and using a keyboard, using a database for hypothesis testing and printing graphs. Most importantly, the use of a database allowed extensive testing of hypotheses formulated by the pupils. This would have been impossible without IT and led to extensive discussion of possible reasons for the patterns that emerged and for the exceptions too!

Has pupils' data-handling expertise been developed in other subjects?

Going Further

- A laptop computer, with a spreadsheet program like PIPEDREAM, could be used to calculate area, discharge, efficiency and other figures in the field.
- Another software package could be used by pupils to plot channel cross-section from width and depth figures.
- Pupils could report their group site descriptions and limitations using a desk top publishing package.
- Data could also be collected on environmental indicators and pollution, possibly covering statements of attainment in AT5.
- Pupils could go on to develop further individual or group studies using this data-handling package and possibly collecting their own data on streams elsewhere for comparison.
- Compare your hydrology schemes of work with relevant Science ATs. See how links with the Science Curriculum can be fostered.

John Davidson, Exeter School.

Source of case study.

4 Petrol stations

Aim of the study.

To introduce ideas concerning the reasons for growth of economic activities, in particular, locations.

Statements of attainment Human Geography: Gg4/4c, Gg4/5c, Gg4/6c, Gg4/7d , Gg4/8d.
IT - Modelling: Te5/4e, Te5/5d, Te5/6d.

Geography aims:
- to identify patterns, interpret data and draw inferences from evidence;
- to reflect on the knowledge and understanding gained and whether experiences have led pupils to question or change any of their assumptions;
- to explain why economic activities may grow in particular locations;
- to promote economic and industrial understanding;
- to introduce concepts of economic demand, competition and marketing.

IT capability aims
- to analyse patterns and relationships in a simple computer model;
- to establish how the rules operate, to change the data and rules and predict the effects.

Software:
STARS a simulation program in which pupils act as managers of competing petrol stations.

Could you use local examples?

The aim of this classroom exercise and simulation is to consider how location and price factors influence the running of profitable petrol stations. Pupils set the price of petrol and the computer calculates the volume of sales at each of six stations, over four seasons giving results as petrol sales and profit and loss statements. Pupils can revise their strategies to alter the petrol price and adjust the weighting factor between price and location.

Initially, we thought the program was only an exercise in industrial location. However, we began to realise that it had wider application as an aid to understanding tertiary activity within cities. Since we wanted to use the simulation as a learning experience and we wished pupils to 'learn by their mistakes', we decided to keep preparatory work down to a minimum and draw the strings together in the follow-up work.

How does this support AT4?

Pupils were given the map of petrol station locations and briefing information on each as provided in the package. They discussed the relative advantages and disadvantages of each location, considering seasonal traffic flows and the type of customer each would attract.

The school has a computer room with 15 computers. Pupils worked in pairs with three petrol stations each. They each had a record sheet on which to record sales and profit/loss performances over three years.

What implications are there for organisation and resources?

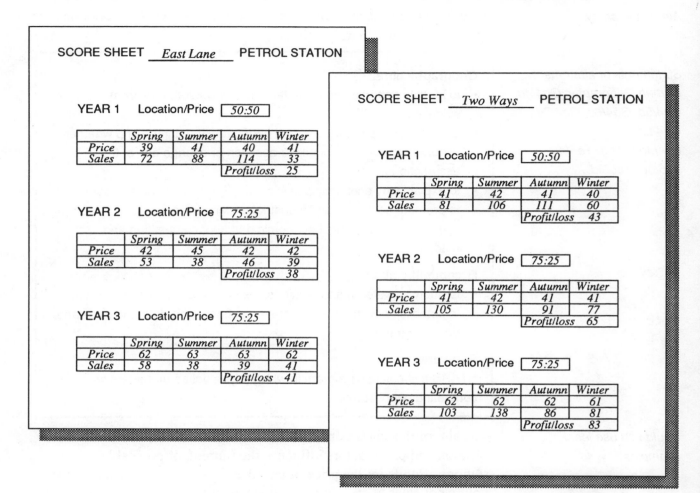

SCORE SHEET __East Lane__ PETROL STATION

YEAR 1   Location/Price 50:50

	Spring	Summer	Autumn	Winter
Price	39	41	40	41
Sales	72	88	114	33
			Profit/loss	25

YEAR 2   Location/Price 75:25

	Spring	Summer	Autumn	Winter
Price	42	45	42	42
Sales	53	38	46	39
			Profit/loss	38

YEAR 3   Location/Price 75:25

	Spring	Summer	Autumn	Winter
Price	62	63	63	62
Sales	58	38	39	41
			Profit/loss	41

SCORE SHEET __Two Ways__ PETROL STATION

YEAR 1   Location/Price 50:50

	Spring	Summer	Autumn	Winter
Price	41	42	41	40
Sales	81	106	111	60
			Profit/loss	43

YEAR 2   Location/Price 75:25

	Spring	Summer	Autumn	Winter
Price	41	42	41	41
Sales	105	130	91	77
			Profit/loss	65

YEAR 3   Location/Price 75:25

	Spring	Summer	Autumn	Winter
Price	62	62	62	61
Sales	103	138	86	81
			Profit/loss	83

Pupils very quickly learnt to use the program without much instruction. The role of the teacher was to advise upon various price-setting strategies if the pupils were confused or continually making losses. However, we hoped that pupils would see the result of their actions and try out various strategies so that by the end of three years they were aware of the attractiveness and potential of these stations.

How could you assess pupils' work?

Pupils approached the exercise with eagerness. The initial attitude was that higher petrol sales must mean more profit, so some entered into a price war, with disastrous results. Many groups were not alert to seasonal changes.. Experience made most very cautious and they decided to keep equal weightings for price and location and experiment with different prices of petrol. By the end of the second year these groups were beginning to show a steady if not spectacular profit at most petrol stations.

Do you make groups competitive?

What is the teacher's role?

For some pupils a small profit was not enough, so they experimented with the weighting factors. One pair set location factors as 100% important and made spectacular profits (unrealistic, but it did highlight the importance of location). Points such as this were noted for follow-up group discussion.

Teacher advice was minimal and consisted of listening to comments, noting points for later discussion and giving advice - at times unwanted, as most pupils felt that they were on the right track and knew better (and occasionally they were proved right).

What self-evaluation task would you prepare?

The lesson proved a very enjoyable and rewarding experience for pupils which I doubt if pupils will forget. However, pupils did accumulate a lot of paper information in front of them and delays in recording information did frustrate some of the budding capitalists. Pupils were asked to write their own evaluation of the lesson and made comments such as 'I learned something that I did not know before', 'location is more influential than price', 'location and price have to be co-ordinated in the right ratio to make a profit', 'is profit the only goal in life'.

What are the key issues for debriefing:
* *Geography?*
* *IT?*
* *Economic awareness*

The follow up lesson was the next day, and we discussed the common strategies that were adopted and the results of more extreme ones. Pupils used the data they had recorded from the program to draw graphs to show sales trends over the three years under different circumstances. Many showed they had developed a basic understanding of location and price determinism. They were asked to think of other retail outlets which might face similar location/price problems and several highlighted the competition between hypermarkets, supermarkets and the corner shop.

We then went on to investigate what other factors might affect the success of a firm, to bring out the more complex issues. This program was a useful way into this topic.

Going further
* Pupils could move from this simple price/location computer simulation to a more advanced one perhaps modelling demographic change or a physical process.
* Pupils could be introduced to the use of spreadsheets for financial planning.

Source of case study.

Adapted from Learning Geography with Computers, NCET 1990.

---

5   Traffic in town

To consider the problem of traffic congestion in a town and suggests alternative solutions.

Aim of Study.

Geography aims:
- to measure and observe outside the classroom;
    - to organise and present the data;
    - to interpret the findings,
    - to offer explanations and conclusions supported by evidence;
    - to evaluate the methods used.
- to examine the effects of changes in the home region.

IT capability aims:
- to use IT for investigations requiring the analysis of data;
- to use a computer model of a situation to form and test simple hypotheses.

Software:
- Any spreadsheet, in this example GRASSHOPPER was used.

Statements of attainment Geographical skills: Gg1/7c. Places: Gg2/4c; Gg2/4d. Human Geography: Gg4/4c, Gg4/4e, Gg4/5d, Gg4/6d, Gg4/7c, Gg4/9b. IT: Te5/4b, Te5/4f, Te5/5d, Te5/6c, Te5/6d, Te5/6e, Te5/7e, Te5/7f, Te5/8d.

Boston, in Lincolnshire, like many other towns, suffers from traffic congestion. A relief road had been built but congestion can still occur in peak periods. The focus of this fieldwork enquiry was the question: 'How can problems of congestion be solved'?

Could you develop this idea in your own area?

As part of their GCSE coursework, students carried out a traffic census at various times of the day at selected points along one route. They used a recording sheet and the teacher prepared a spreadsheet similar in layout to the recording sheet (see overpage). In fact, the recording sheet was prepared from the spreadsheet. Entered into the spreadsheet are scores for Passenger Car Units (PCUs) and traffic saturation levels for various types of road (The scores were from the Department of Transport).

Could this be a student planned enquiry?

Students returned from fieldwork with large amounts of data. They entered the results of their tally counts into the prepared spreadsheet. This did the calculations and gave PCU scores for each vehicle type, PCU scores per hour for each vehicle type and the total traffic flow in PCUs per hour. By studying these figures, students could identify the traffic problem. The morning rush-hour produced traffic flows well in excess of saturation. From the field visit, students recognised the noise problems this had caused and the access problems to terraced houses lining the street.

Is a field visit essential?

Measuring the volume of traffic

How busy is your road?

A Use a recording sheet to count the number of different types of vehicle passing your survey point in 15 minutes (1/4 hour).

B Each type of vehicle has a different score, called Passenger Car Units (PCUs).

VehicleType	PCU value
Bicycles	1/2 point
Motorbikes	1/2 point
Cars	1 point
Vans and minibuses	2 points
Lorries and buses	3 points

C Multiply the number of each vehicle type by its PCU value and total the results to find the Traffic volume in PCUs.

D Multiply the total by 4 to give the PCUs per hour.

Saturation levels

A Different roads can cope with different volumes of traffic.

B The Ministry of Transport has given the maximum PCUs per hour each type of road can cope with.

Road type	Saturation level (PCUs per hour)
7.3m wide (2 lane road)	375
10.0m wide (3 lane road)	688
14.0m wide (dual carriageway)	1512
Motorway	3024

C Decide which type of road you are surveying and compare your volume measured with the Saturation level.

The students were then faced with the problem of seeking a solution to Boston's traffic congestion.

During discussions they made suggestions such as: widening the road, banning commercial vehicles (either lorries or vans), preventing cars turning left and reducing traffic by half. Each of these solutions could then be tested by changing one or more variables in the spreadsheet. Pupil's could immediately see the effects on saturation at different times and at different survey points.

How does IT help the task?

	A	B	C	D	E	F
00:	**Traffic Survey Results Sheet**					
01:						
02:	Date:	10th May 1988		Name:	ABB	
03:						
04:	Town:	Boston	Road:	Fydell St.	Rd. width m	7
05:						
06:	Time: from	9.00	to:	9.15	Max PCU:	375
07:	(15 min.s)				see below	
08:						
09:	Vehicle:	Bicycle	Motorbike	Car	Van /Minibus	Lorry/Bus
10:	PCU value	0.5	0.5	1	2	3
11:						
12:	Traffic count	50	8	60	20	10
13:	PCU score	25	4	60	40	30
14:	PCU/hour:	100	16	240	160	120
15:						
16:	Total PCU/hour: 636					
17:						
18:	Traffic flow:	OK/Too high	* MaxPCU			
19:						
20:		Road width m	Max PCU			
21:		7.3	375			
22:		10.0	688			
23:		14.0	1512			

Groups of students readily tested their ideas and with the aid of graphic displays from the computer they were able to discuss their preferred solutions. This task proved to be well within the capabilities of the pupils and generated excellent discussion about the alternative solutions.

Is the task suitable for a range of activities?

Pupils were keen to experiment with data manipulation and were delighted they did not have to work out all the calculations, and got accurate results every time! On this occasion the formulæ were entered into the spreadsheet by the teacher in advance of the activity, although the calculations were explained and easily understood by the students. However, it is hoped that in the future, when students are already acquainted with spreadsheets, they should be able to set them up for their own enquiries.

Going further

Pupils could:
- word process letters to the planning department outlining their preferred solution;
- produce a newspaper report around this or another planning issue using word processing or a DTP package;
- be given different roles in which to undertake this task, e.g. lorry driver, elderly retired, mother of young children;
- create a spreadsheet model for themselves;
- consider the advantages & disadvantages of different forms of transport.

Source of case study.

Adapted from Alan Bilham-Boult, Traffic in Towns, Planning I.T. in Field Studies, NCET 1990.

---

6 Locating an airport

To consider the effects a new airport would have on an area.

Aim of the study.

Geography aims:
- how conflicting views can arise over the use of land;
- analyse how decisions are taken and may change a region.

IT capability aims:
- to review and discuss their use of IT and consider applications in the outside world;
- modify the data and the rules of a computer model.

Software and resources:
The Choosing Sites package, with the accompanying file on locating an airport.

Statement of attainment.
Places: Gg2/4c.
Human Geography:
Gg4/4e, Gg4/5c, Gg4/5e,
Gg 4/7c, Gg4/8b.
Environmental Geography:
Gg5/6c, Gg5/10a.
IT: Te5/4e, Te5/5d, Te5/6d,
Te5/6e, Te5/7e, Te5/7f.

This study took place over two double lessons. The pupils were organised into groups of two or three and used two computers in the classroom.

I introduced the class to the program and the task, but once the lesson was underway, there was no further teacher-led discussion. My role was to assist with problems and points which groups discovered. I became more of a roving adviser and facilitator than a traditional classroom teacher.

How does this teacher see her role?

Before groups used the computer they had to identify the advantages and disadvantages of a new airport, and consider the factors that were important in deciding where to locate one. Then they had to consider the choices for London's new airport. They were given eight factors and asked to rank them in order and justify their rankings. Many groups reflected the influence of environmental factors from their previous work. They studied descriptions of the five possible sites for the airport and decided which site best suited their ranking.

How does this support AT5?

Once this had been done, they could move to the computer to enter their information and decisions. This initial task had the effect of differentiating the groups. Some worked quickly and superficially, others more slowly and methodically. This meant that there were a steady supply of groups reaching the stage of wanting to use the computer, rather than a rush of several groups all at once. The first group had reached this stage by the end of the first double lesson.

How would you arrange access to computers?

Did the motivation to use IT cause a problem?

The second lesson proceeded in the same way but groups were at different stages in the exercise and were making different demands on me. The first groups rushed their work to be first on the machine, made a poor choice of site and were disgruntled to find there was a better site than the one they had chosen. Other groups thought more carefully about the sites and made better decisions.

The later groups fell into two sorts, those less involved in the work and those which needed lots of help but thought hard about what they were doing. I spent some time with this category. One of the weakest groups in the class was slow but was one of the most successful in making the best decision each time they went to the computer.

What advantages are there in using IT?

If the choice of site made by the group was not the best, they had to reconsider the site descriptions and choose an alternative, returning to the computer to assess this site when the machine was available. If the best site was chosen, they were asked to think about the problem from different points of view; first as a conservationist and then as a government minister, when deciding where to locate the airport.

What non-computing activities could be planned?

When groups reached this stage there was a great deal of necessary movement around the room to and from the computer. It was important to have alternative but relevant tasks to occupy any 'waiting' time. Follow-up work was introduced, which took the form of a report on the groups' work and decisions.

Are computers a real planning tool?

At the end of the second lesson, I led a discussion about the implications of the exercise, in which it was pointed out that no one site had emerged as clear favourite and that the site chosen depended on one's point of view. The computer use was related to the type of software tools that could be used for making similar planning decisions in the real world. The likelihood of conflict between different groups, each with its own views, also was highlighted.

Is the task appropriate for a wide range of abilities?

The tasks were within pupils' capabilities and they understood what they were doing. I was particularly pleased with the results of the weaker groups. Although their exercise was not completed, the groups made good decisions and derived satisfaction from their achievements.

Going further
- The INSITE editor in Choosing Sites can be used to develop a new exercise. Eg. where to locate a nuclear waste dump?
- Involve the IT co-ordinator so that pupils could write their own exercise, thereby providing a geography context for pupils to develop modelling aspects of IT capability.

Source of case study.

Adapted from Learning Geography with Computers, NCET 1990)

7   Data logging: weather

A data logging device, in this case the Weather Reporter is used to record weather data for using in enquiry work and hypothesis testing by pupils.

Aim of study.

Geography Aims:

To use a data logging weather station to collect and store hourly and daily data which pupils can retrieve, display and use for investigating weather patterns and testing hypotheses.

IT Capability Aims:

- to use a computer to obtain remotely sensed data and then store it on disk for later investigation;

- to use a spreadsheet to display, analyse and present conclusions about the patterns and relationships found in the weather data.

Resources:

- Weather Reporter (a data logging weather station) available from the Advisory Unit for Microtechnology in Education, Endymion Road, Hatfield, Herts AL10 8AU;

- a suitable computer with a serial port.

---

*Statements of Attainment
Skills: Gg 1/4d, Gg1/6e.
Physical: Gg 3/4a, Gg3/5a, Gg3/5b.
IT Capability: Te 5/5a, Te5/5d, Te5/6a, Te5/6b, Te5/7c.*

The Weather Reporter is a data-logging weather station. It is mounted on our classroom roof - like an aerial - and is connected to most types of computer via the serial port. In our case we have used both Nimbus 186 and 286 machines. The station automatically stores both hourly and daily data (including rainfall, temperature, wind speed and direction and light intensity), which can be retrieved at will and displayed with simple-to-use software. The data may also be exported to Quest, Grass and Key databases as well as a common format for other packages. We have been using Microsoft EXCEL to display and complete the simple analysis mentioned below.

Do you have a suitable, safe site in your school?

The wealth of data obtained using the Weather Reporter can be a major stimulus for related IT applications. The work based on this topic has been carried out with a number of year eight classes using one or two computers in the room. The pupils follow an investigation of local weather patterns during the Summer term starting with their own questions such as 'On how many days did it rain in June?', 'Does it rain more in the mornings than the afternoons?' and 'What was the hottest day of the term?' Then pupils move on to hypotheses like 'Rainfall is more likely on days with South Westerly winds.' A spreadsheet being used to analyse statistics and to produce charts.

How would you organise storage of this data for later use?

Can activities be designed for different age and ability groups?

How could this work by pupils be assessed?

How could you exchange data with schools in your local area?

Using Microsoft Excel, I have designed a data capture sheet so that students can manually transfer the data into EXCEL I have also developed some Excel macros to automate this process, so that even the less able pupil can produce stunning display charts. Weather reports have provided an excellent starting point for desk-top publishing - for example cutting and pasting charts from EXCEL to WORD FOR WINDOWS to illustrate a written forecast. The students have worked in groups to produce daily summaries and charts and some forecasts which have been posted up in the school each day. These have created a considerable amount of interest as they are outside where the students queue for lunch and are often talking about the weather anyway.

In addition to simply monitoring the weather, other pupils at the school have been using the Weather Reporter to test the accuracy of forecasting. They have compared TV and radio forecasts with the actual recorded weather over a series of days. From this developed a discussion about the differences between local, regional and national weather patterns and this progressed to the idea of micro-climates.

A number of schools in Surrey have Weather Reporters and we have started to exchange data using Electronic Mail. We have set up a bulletin board in the County and schools can upload and download the data at will. In our school the use of the weather reporter has provided an excellent method of introducing information technology quite painlessly and now that the teachers are becoming more IT literate they are looking to branch out into the use of other IT applications such as databases.

Going Further

Schools can explore the use of fax machines for swapping data. This could encourage the study of local weather patterns and pupils could try to track depressions or storms as they cross the county or local area.

- Compare today's weather with that of last year: start an archive of weather data to study long-term trends and patterns.
- See how your schemes of work on weather compare with the work of the Science Department. Can links with the Science curriculum be developed?

Source of case study.

Keith Whiddon, IT Advisory Teacher, Rydens School, Surrey.

---

8 Farm study

To investigate farming, following a fieldwork visit, with the aid of a spreadsheet.

Aim of the study.

Geography aims:
- to look at contrasting types of farm;
- to study factors affecting crop choice on farms;
- investigate how weather and other factors affect crop yields.

IT capability aims:
- to enter data into a spreadsheet;
- to use spreadsheet to test hypotheses and simple modelling.

Software and resources:
- any spreadsheet, such as GRASSHOPPER;
- data on field sizes, crops and yields for local farms.

Statement of attainment.
Places: Gg2/3d, Gg2/5c, Gg2/6a.
Human Geography: Gg4/4e, Gg5/5e.
IT capability: Te5/4c, Te5/5c, Te5/5d, Te5/6d.

'As part of my school's programme of work we make an annual, residential trip to Dyfed. The choice of site is made to allow the children to contrast it with their local environment. We stay very close to a mixed farm where the eloquent and loquacious farmer Bobby Morgan loves to chat to the children. Give him an inch and he will tell children tales of the sea, of the land and, above all, of his farm. During one visit the children happened to ask him about his crops and why he sowed certain crops that are not often seen in Northamptonshire. After a long session where he held the attention of the children in a way which would have gained the admiration of the wisest headteacher, we were armed with statistics about his farm.

How would this help you to deliver AT2?

On our return to Northamptonshire we were able to compare these with statistics about our local farm. All the usual studies were made and data collected. Then I introduced my old geographical farming game where the children were set the task of running an arable farm over a three-year period. Dice were thrown, cards were drawn, and the calculator buttons pressed until they cried out for mercy. The children who were finding the calculations beyond them were soon attracting my attention more than those who were ploughing on (pardon the pun).

Then came a blinding revelation. Why not use a spreadsheet? If the spreadsheet could do away with the calculations, then we would achieve the concepts we were striving to engender.

Is prior knowledge of spreadsheets necessary?

Are there other strategies for introducing formulæ which you could use?

Across the top row of the spreadsheet we fed in the names of the fields. Under each field name we entered the hectarage. We had three main crops under consideration: potatoes, cereals and grass. We had been told that not only did the soil affect the yield, but other factors such as the stone content and the proximity to the sea cliffs. I had already entered the formulæ with a group of the more mathematically able, and as soon as the yield was entered the calculations were completed. Each field now had a total, dependent upon the crop that had been sown. Looking along the totals for each field, we were able to see those with the poorest yield.

What questions would you suggest?

Could they be improved by sowing an alternative crop? Try it, and the tedious recalculations are done instantly by the spreadsheet. Of course, some children pointed out that, whatever crop we sow, we cannot increase the total for that field because it was small to start with. However, by producing line graphs of the field size and an overlay of the totals, we can instantly see which fields are below standard. A whole rich area of language followed when the children tried to gain the optimum total.

What other follow up work with spreadsheets could you do?

How can pupil work be assessed?

The children continued using the spreadsheet to investigate the effects of the weather, the consequences of a glut in production and the need for a crop rotation.'

Throughout their work, the calculations took a back seat and the decision-making came to the fore. By the teacher's choice in this particular piece of work, the pupils were not involved in the mathematics of programming the spreadsheet. Their mathematical involvement came from seeking optimum solutions and experimenting with very many 'What if?' questions.

Going further

Pupils could:

- develop their own fieldwork enquiry for a local farm and design their own spreadsheet to analyse data and explore 'What if?' questions;
- look at implications of changing farming patterns such as the 'set aside' scheme, or conversion from pasture to arable, and use a spreadsheet to model possible consequences.

Source of case study.

Focus on I.T., NCET 1991. This case study first appeared in Micromath, Spring 1989 and also appears in 'Thinking about Spreadsheets (NCET 1990).

---

9   Changes in the shopping centre

To use an enquiry approach to study changes in a local shopping centre.

Aim of study.

Geography aims:
- to identify key issues concerning shop location and shopping patterns in the home region;
- to look at landuse & shopping patterns by local fieldwork enquiry;
- to present results of the enquiry to an audience.

IT capability aims:
- to use data-handling package to explore, organise & present data;
- to use dtp / word processing package to present findings.

Software and resources:
- any suitable data handling package such as, GRASS or EXCEL;
- dtp or word processing package.

Statement of attainment.
Skills: Gg1/5d.
Places: Gg2/3e, Gg2/3f, Gg2/4c, Gg2/4d, Gg2/6a.
Human Geography: Gg4/3d, Gg4/4b, Gg4/4c, Gg4/5c, Gg4/5e, Gg4/6b, Gg4/7b.
Environmental: Gg5/3b.
IT capability: Te5/3a, Te5/3c, Te5/4a, Te5/4c, Te5/5a, Te5/5c, Te5/6a, Te5/6c, Te5/7a, Te5/7d.

The Statutory Order for Geography states 'an enquiry approach should be adopted for classroom activities, and work outside the classroom should be undertaken where appropriate.' (Programmes of Study at Key Stage 3) Enquiry is also highlighted at Key Stages 2 and 4. Information Technology has a key role in the enquiry process. The flow diagram opposite outlines some of the opportunities for using IT in a geographical enquiry. Several of the earlier case studies also have used IT within an enquiry approach.

The table overpage shows how a teacher of geography planned a fieldwork enquiry on a shopping centre for year 9 pupils. The use of IT was fully integrated as the geography department had agreed to help deliver the IT capability strands of Communicating Ideas and Handling Information for Key Stage 3. As a result, the geography department had the use of IT awareness periods during the course of this enquiry.

How could you make use of IT awareness periods in your school?

The shopping centre was undergoing major changes. Redevelopment proposals affected smaller shops and the centre was competing with new, edge of town superstores. In the enquiry, pupils had to:
- identify the key issues;
- look at present landuses and shopping patterns;
- collect information on proposed changes;
- evaluate effects of possible changes.

IT and the route for enquiry

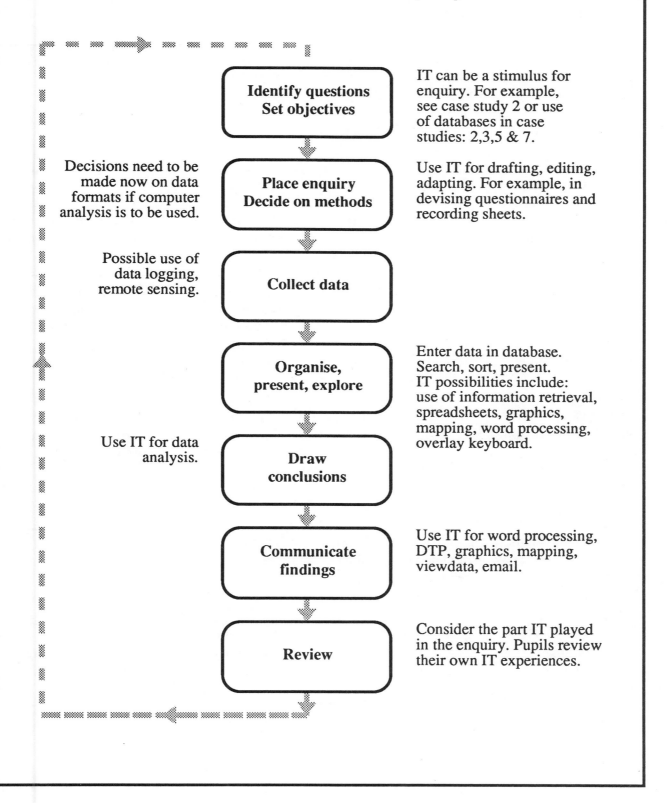

**Identify questions
Set objectives**

IT can be a stimulus for enquiry. For example, see case study 2 or use of databases in case studies: 2,3,5 & 7.

Decisions need to be made now on data formats if computer analysis is to be used.

**Place enquiry
Decide on methods**

Use IT for drafting, editing, adapting. For example, in devising questionnaires and recording sheets.

Possible use of data logging, remote sensing.

Collect data

Organise, present, explore

Enter data in database. Search, sort, present. IT possibilities include: use of information retrieval, spreadsheets, graphics, mapping, word processing, overlay keyboard.

Use IT for data analysis.

Draw conclusions

Communicate findings

Use IT for word processing, DTP, graphics, mapping, viewdata, email.

Review

Consider the part IT played in the enquiry. Pupils review their own IT experiences.

Planning a shopping enquiry

Stage / timing	Geography activities	Enquiry skills	IT activities and capabilities
Pre-enquiry. 3 lessons.	Key questions for enquiry on shopping patterns. Plus changes identified by pupils, parents and teachers pooling knowledge.	Identify topics. Suggest key geographical questions.	
Plan on enquiry. Decide on methods. 2 lessons & IT awareness time.	Planning of timescale, data collection, interviews and mapping.	Identify information required. Decide on methods.	Data collection structured to make data suitable for entry into data-handling package.
Data collection. 1 day.	Fieldwork and use of libraries.	Make accurate observations and measurements. Select relevant information from sources.	Questionnaires and recording sheets prepared on computer.
Organise /present / explore information. 3 lessons & IT awareness time.	Enter relevant data into data-handling package. Print out graphs and tables. Role-play to explore data.	Identify and describe patterns. Explore geographical relationships.	Data-handling package used to organise, present and explore data.
Draw conclusions. 2 lessons & IT awareness time.	Identify broad picture of changes. Consider reasons for them and the implications.	Use evidence to support explanations.	
Communicate findings. 1 lesson & IT awareness time.	Present findings. Oral presentation, wall display, leaflets, reports.	Present coherent accounts.	DTP / word processing packages used by pupils.
Review. 1 lesson.	Reflect on methods. Look at strengths and weaknesses.	Evaluate methods.	Review and discuss use and values of IT.

What opportunities are there for summative assessment through wall displays, oral presentations or written reports and leaflets?

How could this be linked to formal assessment?

Pupils worked in groups and it was important to identify the role individuals took within each group. The teacher observed pupils at work, and informally discussed with individuals the decisions taken and conclusions reached. At the end of the enquiry, pupils communicated their findings and reviewed their experiences.

Pupil self-evaluation checklist

In this enquiry you will study:
- how to set up and carry out a geographical enquiry;
- some of the geographical and IT skills used in enquiry;
- how and why shopping centres are changing;
- the effects of shopping centre changes on different people and interest groups in the community.

Tick the boxes when you have completed the following work:

Did you: ☑

1   Identify changes in the shopping centre ☐
2   List sources of data that could be used for enquiry? ☐
3   Collect primary data during fieldwork? ☐
4   Collect secondary data? ☐
5   Enter some of this data into the computer? ☐
6   Draw graphs or diagrams to present data? ☐
7   Search the database to help identify patterns? ☐
8   Identify how changes in the shopping centre have affected different people and interest groups? ☐
9   Present your findings with the aid of a computer? ☐
10 Learn about strengths and weaknesses of data collection and databases? ☐

To help assess their individual contributions to the group task, pupils completed an evaluation checklist. This involved them in assessment and evaluation, giving them some responsibility for it. So pupils knew what they were trying to achieve and recognised what they had learnt.

Going further

Pupils could:
- develop their own fieldwork enquiry for a local row of shops and design their own data collection methods using IT.

Teachers could:
- develop pupil self evaluation sheets for other case studies;
- reflect on IT work for years 7 and 8 before this work in year 9.

Source of case study.

David Leat, School of Education, University of Newcastle.